DEVONSHIRE JOKES AND STORIES

COMPILED BY JAMES WHINRAY

"Believe nothing of what you hear
and only half of what you see."

Popular Devon saying

TOR MARK PRESS · PENRYN

The Tor Mark series

Folklore

Other titles

First published 1996 by Tor Mark Press,
Islington Wharf, Penryn, Cornwall TR10 8AT
© 1996 Tor Mark Press
ISBN 0-85025-354-3
The cover illustration is by Beryl Sanders
Printed in Cornwall, UK, by Cornwall Litho, Redruth

Some Devonshire jokes

A parson called one day at an outlying cottage to sympathize with an elderly workman on the death of his wife, and found him working in his garden. After some words from the parson, the old man leaned on his fork and philosophized:
'I dur zay zome 'ud think I'd be indoors a-mournin'! An zo I'd like to be. But what I do zay, Pa'son, is, business fust an' pleasure a'terwards!'

A very stout woman was always accounting for her obesity as she waddled up and down the village by telling her neighbours: 'There! I've had a deal of troubles in me time, and they'm all turned in'ards I s'pose.'

A certain Peter was taken ill and died. The local Lady Bountiful called to condole with the widow. 'So you have lost your good man?'
'Iss,' replied Betty, 'Peter's gone to Beelzebub's bosom.'
'Pshaw,' replied the visitor, 'you don't know what you're talking about.'
'P'raps I don't,' answered Betty placidly. 'Peter and me never could mind the names of great folks.'

A landowner went to an Exeter lawyer in great alarm. 'That scoundrel — — has forged a Mortgage on my land!' 'Don't worry, we can always forge a Reconveyance.'

A man was making his way through Aune Mire when he came upon a top hot reposing brim downwards on the sedge. He stirred it with his foot, whereupon a voice called out from beneath, 'What be y'a-doin' to my 'at?'
The man replied, 'Be there now a chap under 'en?'
'Ees, I reckon,' was the reply, 'and a hoss under me likewise.'

A young farmer was taking a Sunday school class.
'Now, Tom, what is your duty to your neighbour?'
'My duty to my neighbour,' faltered Tom, 'is to believe in him.'
'No, no, Tom, that will never do. Your duty to your neighbour is to love him as yourself. You may love him as much as you please, Tom, but don't you believe in him, for if you believe in him, he will do you, Tom, for certain.'

An old woman in a village composed songs, and sang them. The curate jestingly invited her to sing a duet with him at the next village concert. She accepted with alacrity. 'You shall sing counter-alto, sir,' she said, 'and I'll sing terrible.'

The land steward, or as we should now call him, estate manager, was never popular, especially if he was a hard man. There were exceptions, of course. One such died, and the tenants subscribed to a memorial in the parish church,

A STEWARD AND A JUST MAN.

A tenant from a neighbouring estate studied the inscription carefully, and then said, 'However did'm get both into the one coffin?'

A man was loading hay onto a wagon, when suddenly he realised that he was high up and there was no way down without breaking his neck. The ladder had been taken away, and the waggon was on the move and swaying. He shouted down to the farmer, 'Here I be, sure enough maister, but how be I to get down?'

'Oh, if thee shuts thee eyes and walks about a bit, thee'll cum down vast enough.'

A North Devon farmer, and churchwarden, said he knew for certain that the clergy attended episcopal visitations in order to swop sermons under the eye of the bishop; and he added slyly, 'Our parson got a terrible poor set last year.'

'Where be going with the lantern, John,' asks the farmer of a young labourer hurrying down the lane.

'Going courting, maister.'

'What do 'ee want a lantern vur?'

'To zee what I be doin', maister.'

'Tut man, I never took a lantern when I went a-courting.'

'That's what I thought, maister, when I fust zeed the missis,' says John, walking off.

A husband took his second wife to see the grave of his first. When they came to the spot, he innocently asked, 'Do you not think, my dear, that the inscription is very appropriate?'

'You mean,' she replied, 'BE YOU ALSO READY?'

'What is higher than Yes Tor?'

'Why, no tor.'

(A joke unkindly ruined by the surveyors, who declare neighbouring High Willhays to be 3 metres higher.)

Epitaph formerly in Bideford churchyard:

> Here lies the body of Mary Sexton
> Who pleased many a man
> But never vexed one –
> Unlike the woman under the next stone.

Out of the way of the world's stresses, rural Devonians were famously long-lived. A tourist once met an old man, sobbing bitterly into his white beard.

'Why do you cry, my man?' he asked.

'Feyther hev been a-beating me,' blubbered the old fellow.

'Father been beating you?' echoed the astonished visitor. 'What on earth for?'

'For throwing stones at gran'feyther,' whined the old man.

Kill'em or Cure'em Budd

Dr John Wreyford Budd practised in Plymouth. He was a man of rough manners, blunt and to the point in all he said, and there are many anecdotes about him.

A fellow doctor, passing Dr Budd's house, was startled by the sudden descent of a leg of mutton into the street, flung out of the window by the irate doctor, because somewhat overdone. He would often, when giving a dinner party, rise at the conclusion of the first courses saying, 'I shan't take any sweets,' would go to the fireside and fill a long 'churchwarden' clay, then, leaning against the mantlepiece, calmly smoke and join in the conversation of the guests as they continued at table.

A friend took Budd out in his yacht. As the vessel skimmed through the smooth waters of Plymouth Sound, 'He's a fool, a cursed fool,' said Budd, 'who has the means and don't keep a yacht.'

Presently the boat shot out beyond the breakwater and began to pitch. 'He's a fool, a cursed fool,' said he, 'who, having the means, keeps a yacht; and he's a cursed fool who, having a friend that has a yacht, allows himself to be over-persuaded to go out with him.'

As a doctor, Budd broke through the wretched system that then prevailed of bleeding and giving lowering diet for every kind of malady. 'Chuck the slops away, and chuck the doctors after them, with their pills and lancets,' he thundered. 'Give the patient three or four glasses of champagne a day, a bowl of beef-tea every three hours, beefsteaks, mutton-chops and oysters.'

A girl was shown to him in a sort of box, almost like a coffin. He had been called in to examine her, and he said that he would undertake to cure her if she were taken to his house and his treatment were not interfered with.

'But, oh! Doctor,' said the mother, 'dearest Evangeline can eat nothing but macaroons.'

'In-Deed!'

'And, oh! Doctor, she cannot bear the light; and the shutters have to be kept fast, and even the blinds down. The least ray of light causes her excruciating pain.'

'Ha! Humph!'

'And, Dr Budd, she cannot stand; she lies always in that box; and what is more, she can't speak, only moans and mutters.'

'I understand. Send her to me.'

So the box was brought. To accommodate it a hearse was hired – no cab or carriage would contain it in a horizontal position. The chest with the hysterical girl in it was carried into one of Budd's rooms in his house, where the shutters were closed and the curtains drawn.

The weeping mother departed after giving strict injunctions to the doctor not to allow any noise to be made in the house, no doors to be slammed, or poor darling Evangeline would go into convulsions – so highly strung were her sensitive nerves.

'Humph!' said Budd, and saw the good lady depart. He allowed ten minutes to elapse, and then he went upstairs, stamping on every step, threw open the door of the room in which his patient lay, and shouted –

'Halloo! What tomfoolery is this? I'll soon make an end to it.' He went to the window, drew back the curtains, threw open the shutters, and let the sun stream into the apartment. The girl began to moan and cry.

'Stop that nonsense,' said he. 'I'm not like that fool of a mother of yours to believe in your whims. Get out of that box this instant.'

The girl began to tremble, but made no attempt to obey.

Budd went to a drawer and pulled out a pistol. Then to a cupboard and emptied a draught into a glass.

'Now then,' said he, 'which shall it be, pistol or poison? I'll gripe you with the dose till you squeal with good reason, or put a bullet into you, whichever you prefer. It's all one to me, but out of that box you jump.'

And jump she did, and fell on her knees before Budd. 'Oh! please, please, do not kill me!'

'I am not going to kill you if you do what you're told. Sit down there.'

The girl did so. He rang the bell and when a servant appeared he ordered a beefsteak and a small bottle of porter, and bread. These were speedily brought into the room.

'Now then, eat and drink and enjoy yourself.'

'I – I – I can only eat macaroons.'

'Macaroons be damned. You eat that steak and drink that

porter,' roared Budd, 'or…' and he proceeded to cock and present the pistol.

The girl tremblingly obeyed, but presently became interested in the succulent beef and some crisp potatoes, and the porter she sipped first, and then drank, and drained the tumbler.

'That will do for today,' said Budd. 'I have sent for your out-of-door clothes, and tomorrow morning you shall trundle a hoop round Princess Square. Now I'll leave you a packet of illustrated books. You dine with me this evening at seven.'

A small girl had a tiresome nervous cough. Dr Budd was called in. He heard her cough. Then he suddenly took her up in his arms and planted her on the mantleshelf.

'There!' said he. 'Balance yourself here for half an hour.' He pulled out his watch. 'If you cough, you will infallibly tumble over among the fire-irons and cut your head. You are a nice little girl, you are an active little girl, you are a pretty little girl; but you have one cussed fault which makes every one hate you, and I'm going to cure you of that. No coughing. The fire is burning, and if you do fall I suspect your skirt will catch fire, and you will be frightfully burnt, besides having your cheek cut open by the fender.'

A Dartmoor farmer came to Dr Budd one day, suffering from congestion of the lungs. 'You go home and to bed at once,' said Dr Budd. 'And here's a draught for you to take internally, and here are some leeches to be applied externally.'

'Please, your honour, to write it down,' said John.

'Can you read?'

'Yes, I reckon, but my Mary can't.'

So Dr Budd wrote the instructions. A fortnight later, the same patient called again. He was recovered.

'Well,' said the doctor, 'you took my prescriptions?'

'Aye, I reckon I did – and drashy things they were.'

'You put the leeches on?'

'I reckon I put them in, sir. I read what you'd wrote and we understood you to say that they was to be fried, so my Mary, her put the pan on the fire, and a pat o' butter and a shred o' onion, and fried 'em, live as they were. But Lord! for mussy's sake, doctor, don't ax me to ate any more o' them things. I'd rayther take a whole box o' pills all to wance.'

A gentleman called on him one day just before Budd sat down to dinner, and brought with him his brother, suffering from lock-jaw.

'I'm not going to be interfered with at my dinner for you or the

King,' said Budd; then to his servant: 'Here, George, lay two plates for these gentlemen, the one who can't speak place opposite me at the bottom of the table, and for the other gentleman in the middle on my left.'

Whether they would or no, the two visitors were obliged to comply; they knew the imperious nature of the doctor, and that unless he were humoured, he would kick them out of the house and refuse to attend to the patient.

A roast leg of mutton was placed before Dr Budd; he proceeded to carve a great slice, then took it and threw the slab of meat in the face of the gentleman on his left, who staggered back and hastily seized his napkin to wipe his face and sweep the juice from his shirt-front and waistcoat. But before he had cleansed himself, slap came another slice of mutton in his face, and then a third. At this the man with the lock-jaw burst into a roar of laughter.

'There,' said Budd, 'I have cured you; you will have to pay for a new waistcoat for your brother, it's messed with grease.'

Budd was visiting a farmer in the country. Every time he left, a prentice boy on the farm came with an anxious face to inquire how his master was. The doctor was touched at the intense interest the lad took in the condition of his master. One day as he left, and the boy asked after the farmer, Budd shook his head and said, 'I fear it's going bad with him.'

The lad burst into a loud boohoo of tears and sobs.

'There, there,' said the doctor, 'don't take on so, my lad. It can't be helped.'

'Oh, you'd take on if you were in my place,' sobbed the youth, 'for missus makes us eat all the stock, pigs and what not, as dies on the farm.'

The Fulford oak

The Fulfords of Great Fulford, about halfway, as the crow flies, between Crediton and Moretonhamstead, held their estates by a strange tenure. Once a year they had to dine in the top of an old oak tree which had been so pollarded that a floor had been laid between its upper branches, and then give a dance there for their tenants.

Sir Walter's wooing

That great Devonian Sir Walter Raleigh was a favourite of Queen Elizabeth, but she liked her favourites to conceal discreetly any feelings they might have for other women, and Raleigh had to leave court when it became known that he had 'devirginated' one of the Queen's Maids of Honour, Elizabeth Throckmorton. The scurrilous John Aubrey (as ever) knew the details:

He loved a wench well; and one time getting one of the Maids of Honour up against a tree in a wood, who seemed at first boarding to be something fearful of her honour, and modest, she cried, 'Sweet Sir Walter, what do you ask me? Will you undo me? Nay, sweet Sir Walter! Sweet Sir Walter! Sir Walter!' At last as the danger and the pleasure at the same time grew higher, she cried in the ecstasy 'Swisser Swatter Swisser Swatter!' She proved with child, and I doubt not but this hero took care of them both, as also that the product was more than an ordinary mortal.

Box and box about

Raleigh did indeed marry the maid, and the son lived long enough to be killed during Raleigh's final expedition to America, but Aubrey also has a story of another of his sons. Sir Walter had been invited to dine at some great person's, and his son with him, so he said to the son, 'Thou art expected today at dinner to go along with me, but thou art such a quarrelsome affronting tarrarag that I am ashamed to have such a bear in my company.'

Mr Walter humbled himself to his father, and promised he would behave himself mighty mannerly. So away they went. He sat next to his father and was very demure at least half dinner time. Then, said he, 'I, this morning, not having the fear of God before my eyes but by the instigation of the devil, went to a whore. I was very eager of her, kissed and embraced her, and went to enjoy her, but she thrust me from her, and vowed I should not, "For your father lay with me but an hour ago."'

Sir Walter, being so strangely surprised and put out of his countenance at so great a table, gives his son a damned blow over the face. His son, as rude as he was, would not strike his father, but strikes over the face the gentleman that sat next to him on the other side and said, 'Box about; 'twill come to my father anon.'

No smoking without fire

Sir Walter is said to have been the first man to introduce tobacco into England. When one of his servants first came into the room and, from behind, saw him apparently on fire, she threw a ewer of water over him to put it out.

Hived off

Superstition demanded that, on the day of a funeral, any bee-hives which had belonged to the deceased were to be turned round. One incident of black comedy arose from a misunderstanding of this custom. At the funeral of a Cullompton farmer, instead of turning the beehives round, a servant who did not understand the custom up-ended them. The bees were of course irate, and attacked the horses and riders; in vain they galloped off, for the bees followed them vigorously. In the general confusion, hats, wigs and dignity were all lost, and the coffin was left unattended for some time, before peace could be restored.

Thicky's the way to Dartmoor

A famously disreputable family called Cheriton lived at Nymet Rowland. No one could beat them at rough horseplay and filthy language. They were a disgrace to their neighbourhood and a nuisance to their neighbours. One passer-by reported that he was accosted by a woman of the tribe who called him disgusting names, pelted him with mud and stones, performed indescribably offensive acts, and finally chased him with a hay fork, at which he beat a hasty retreat.

Their fame grew. Many inquisitive people went to Nymet Rowland to get a peep at the 'savages'. One man approached too near the house and was at once pounced upon by a couple of Amazons, who demanded the reason for his visit. 'Ladies,' said he, 'I have lost my way. Will you put me on the right road for Dartmoor?'

'Aw, eees, tü be sure,' replied Miss Cheriton, 'Come theäse yer way an' I'll shaw'ee.' She took him into the adjoining yard ostensibly to direct him, but the unsuspecting wayfarer, venturing too near the edge of the horse pond in following his guide, was suddenly thrust into the filthy liquid, as a 'There, thicky's the way tü Dartymoor, and be damned tü you,' fell on his ears.

The Mayor of Bradninch returns an answer

In the time when eating and drinking were the chief duties of civic office, a mayor of Exeter sent a polite letter to his counterpart in Bradninch, by special messenger, inviting him to dine. The messenger found his worship of Bradninch on the roof of a house, following his calling as a thatcher. On being informed that there was a note for him, he asked the messenger to bring it up the ladder.

His worship, not being able to read, and there being no town clerk present, opened it and held it before him, pretending to read, and considering what reply to make whilst not knowing the contents or even whom it was from. The messenger, observing that the letter was being held upside down, humbly hinted as much to the mayor. His worship immediately replied, 'How dare you, you impertinent scoundrel, dictate to the Mayor of Bradninch in what way he shall read a letter? Go home to your master, and tell him that when he sends a more discreet and civil messenger, I'll return him an answer.'

To which of you am I betrothed?

The Tremaine family, of Sydenham House near Marystow, not infrequently included twins. At one time, there were two identical girls, one of whom had been on a visit to a friend in the country, where she had won the heart of a young gentleman, who soon became her accepted lover. It was of course necessary for him to obtain her father's consent, and for this purpose he followed her to London. On his arrival, he was shown into a room where the other sister, whom he had never seen, was sitting alone; instantly mistaking her for his betrothed, he addressed her as such. The young lady, who had a mind to keep up the joke, let him continue for a few minutes, when the door opened and in came the other twin. The lover, astonished to find two sweethearts where he expected but one, and not knowing which was the right one, felt himself under the necessity of begging they would be kind enough to tell him to which lady he was engaged.

Rolling in it

The renowned crusader Sir John de Sully returned home after many years' absence. His steward brought in the accounts of his estates, together with the coffer containing his rents, which over that long period had mounted into a great mass of money. He caused his best cloak, which was of cloth of gold, to be unpacked and spread upon the ground, and commanded the money to be put inside it, then cast himself on top of it, so that it might be said that once he had tumbled in gold and silver. Then he divided it, one part to his wife, one part for his servants and household officers, and one part for the poor.

Unusual custom of old Dartmoor

Entry in Parish Register of Mary Tavy, 12 September 1756:

'Robert Elford was baptized, the child of Susanna Elford by her sister's husband, to whom she was married with the consent of the sister, the wife, who was at the wedding.'

The voyage of Cove's bed

In 1537 a flood swelled the Exe so much that in the middle of the night the torrent destroyed a pier of the bridge at Tiverton. Right alongside the bridge was the house of a man named Cove, and as the bridge collapsed it took Cove's house along with it. It was a three storey house and it fell with a great crash; the servants in topmost rooms were all thrown into the river and drowned, but Cove and his wife, sleeping in a lower room, were carried into the water, bed and all. He ordered his wife not to rock the boat, and using sometimes his hands and sometimes his feet instead of oars, kept himself on west side of the river, out of a strong eddy, and at length reached a hillock where the waters were shallow, and he and his wife came ashore safely.

The gallant Mrs Partington

Sydney Smith, a reformist politician of the early nineteenth century, made the following comment on the attempts of the House of Lords to prevent reform of the electoral system, especially the elimination of 'rotten boroughs' from which peers benefited.

'I do not mean to be disrespectful but the attempt of the Lords to stop the progress of reform reminds me very forcibly of the great storm at Sidmouth, and of the conduct of the excellent Mrs Partington on that occasion. In the winter of 1824 there set in a great flood upon that town – the tide rose to an incredible height – the waves rushed in upon the houses, and everything was threatened with destruction. In the midst of this sublime and terrible storm, Dame Partington, who lived upon the beach, was seen at the door of her house with mop and pattens, trundling her mop, squeezing out the sea water, and vigorously pushing away the Atlantic Ocean. The Atlantic was roused. Mrs Partington's spirit was up. But I need not tell you the contest was unequal. The Atlantic Ocean beat Mrs Partington. She was excellent with a slop or a puddle, but she should not have meddled with a tempest.'

A private charity

In North Molton there lived a charitably disposed old lady, one Mrs Passmore, a dressmaker. At Christmas this dear old soul always had ready basins of small coins to be distributed in the shape of doles. The Lady Morley of that period is said to have taken it into her head that this amiable custom detracted in some measure from the honour and reverence due to herself; so she suggested to Mrs Passmore that, as no doubt their charities overlapped, and some people had more than their share while others had nothing, it might be well to entrust her with the combined fund and allow her to act as almoner.

'No, my lady,' was the reply, 'I don't think I will. You know they come and say, "Thank 'ee Lady Morley" and "God bless 'ee Lady Morley!" but if I give away my own money I shall have all the God bless 'ees myself.'

Coffin leaps into grave

The vicars of Bideford were entitled to claim a 'heriot', or death duty, whenever a farmer in the parish died, and this was to consist of the dead man's best cow. This dubious custom probably dated back even before William the Conqueror granted Bideford to the son of Hamo the Toothy.

Sir William Coffin (whose descendants are now the Pine-Coffins) was passing the churchyard one day in 1529 when he observed a commotion. A corpse was awaiting burial. It seemed the priest would not bury it until he had received his heriot, but the dead man had possessed only one cow and no other property, so his widow and children would become destitute. After unsuccessfully trying to reason with the greedy priest, Sir William leapt into the grave, saying to the priest, 'Very well, then, stick me in the grave and cover me up, instead of the corpse; and you can have my second best cow.'

At this the priest thought it might be safer to yield – yet afterwards he complained to the ecclesiastical court and Sir William was charged with violating the privileges of the church. But his court contacts were such that he not only escaped punishment, he even persuaded parliament to improve the law by abolishing such heriots.

Another version of this story says that Sir William put the priest in the grave and almost buried him alive. Take your pick!

The workhouse is where you lay your head

In the days when each parish was responsible for its own paupers, there were many shabby attempts to pass paupers from one parish to another, and as a result many unfortunate men and women suffered even greater hardship than if they had been accepted into their nearest workhouse. One such dispute, however, had its amusing aspect.

Hornshayne House, the home of the Marwood family in the eighteenth century, was situated on the junction of the parish boundaries of Colyton, Southleigh and Farway. In 1765, a servant at the house became a pauper – probably because he could no longer work through age or sickness. Which parish should support him? Colyton was able to claim that only the Hornshayne dairy was in their parish, and the man had not worked in the dairy, so they were not responsible. So it was between Southleigh and Farway. Their lawyers were finally able to agree that the crucial point was where he slept – but his bed lay across the boundary! Back it went to the lawyers, who declared that in such a case the crucial point was where he laid his head to sleep, so two arbitrators went to the house.

It was clear where the parish boundary ran, because in those days 'beating the bounds' was an annual ritual, and every boy in the area knew that the boundary went along the line of a beam through the Hornshayne kitchen. But the servant had his bed in the garret, so surveyors were called in to plot a true perpendicular line from his pillow (once they had taken depositions as to which was the head of the bed and which the foot) down to the kitchen.

And whilst Southleigh had him from the chest downwards, it appeared that Farway had the honour of his head – and so Farway had to maintain him. But they probably spent less in doing so than they had already spent on lawyers' fees!

Stories of the hunting parsons

At the beginning of the nineteenth century, few counties in England produced such a crop of hunting parsons as did Devonshire. Parson Jack Russell was said to be 'a worthy, kind-hearted, God-fearing man,' and our attitude towards him will depend largely on our attitude to hunting, and to the yappy little brutes to which he gave his name! Perhaps he did spend most of his time in the chase, and rather too little at his job, but his flock liked him and he did live among them, which is more than can be said for many of his contemporaries. Parsons Froude and Radford were in a different league entirely. They were both undoubtedly guilty of serious crimes, for which they were never brought to justice. Here are some stories about the three of them, and of Bishop Phillpotts who was consecrated Bishop of Exeter in 1831.

The unspeakable avoiding the ineffable

Shortly after his consecration, as Bishop Phillpotts was driving with his chaplain on the way to a Confirmation, a fox-hunt passed by in full halloo.

'Dear me!' exclaimed his lordship; what a number of black coats among the hunters. Has there been some great bereavement in the neighbourhood?'

'My lord,' replied the chaplain, 'the only bereavement these black-coated sportsmen suffer from is not being able to appear in pink.'

Brotherly love

A dispute arose between Parsons Froude and Russell, stemming from some uncharitable words in the field.

Froude was not the kind of man to 'pass by a matter' even if he were ever so much in the wrong, and the opportunity arose on the way home of trying to vindicate at least his seniority – for he was an older man than Russell. They met again at the top of the narrow lane that leads from Court Down to Dulverton – a very lonely spot with high hedges on either side completely shutting out and shutting in all views and sounds. As his powerful nag was trotting stoutly down through the mud, making loud suction noises with his hooves and spurting up the dirty water on every side, Russell saw Froude ahead of him, dismounted, with his weedy thoroughbred drawn right across the lane, completely blocking his way, and he guessed it foreboded evil. As he drew near, 'Who'th a-made thee into a lecturing Beeshop like mi lord Veel-the-Pot of Exeter, I should like vor knaw?' began Froude. 'While thee's a-got they there blaggard rascals about thee and a vew of the gintry thee canst zay 'at thee'st like I s'pose. 'Tis my turn now! Git off thick there gurt cart 'oss o'thine and I'll taich thee better manners!'

'I will certainly obey you,' replied Russell (getting off his horse and tying his reins to a stump in the hedge), 'since you are my senior by ten years at least. What now?' he added, and turned round and faced him. As he did so, Froude's hunting crop fell in a heavy blow over his shoulder, leaving his ear bleeding and his back tingling from the smartest cut he had ever received since he was at Blundell's School. But the next moment he had gripped the striker, wrested the weapon from his hands, thrown it aside and, with what was among wrestlers called a Lancashire twist, had laid Froude gently and impotently on his back upon the Autumn grass, holding both arms down by the sides and bestriding his legs to keep him from kicking.

How long he would have held him there I do not know, for his task was to keep him in this position until he got into a better temper and on his honour promised to proceed in a peaceable way and acknowledge that the rebuke he had given him was just and right.

But while he was reasoning with him thus, face to face, another hunter came trotting down the lane. When he saw the two horses tied to the hedge, and then looked upon the two parsons, the one struggling and fuming and swearing on the ground, and the other kneeling over his victim and arguing with him in the kindest language, he first of all burst into laughter, and then, when he saw the angry looks of Jack Froude, and Russell's bleeding face: 'Gentlemen, gentlemen!' said he. 'What be you about here? – two brethren of the cloth! Two deputies of peace and good will amongst men! Fighting like two ruffians on the highway! Like two stags in the rutting season! Like two ill-behaved hounds in the hunting field! What would Bishop Phillpotts say if he saw ye now? But if neither of ye would take heed to him – so let me tell ye that Mr Bisset and Lord Ebrington are coming on behind with a number of others, and what a disgrace it will be for them to see you like this! How delighted the Radical papers will be to publish a column with this title, 'Two parsons fighting on the Highway!''

With that Froude gave way and yielded all the other asked him to yield, and they both rose to their feet just as a large party of riders came down the lane. 'What's the matter, Parson Froude?' said Mr Bisset, as they passed. 'Ah! I thought that weedy toad of a horse would come down with ye!'

Froude did not answer.

'Yes,' said Russell, 'but it might have been much worse, Mr Bisset – much worse – much worse! 'Twas an easy fall!'

And then they all laughed together as they rode on – except Froude, and he rode away silent, with the mud still hanging to his red coat and hat.

Unprepare ye the way of the Lord Bishop

On one occasion Bishop Phillpotts planned a visit to Froude, vicar of Knowstone and a man who ruled his locality with a gang of ruffians, who thought nothing of firing a rick at his suggestion, or loosening a carriage wheel so that the driver was spilled.

Froude had no wish to see the bishop, so he had the road dug up. A wide hole was created, into which a marsh would drain. It was covered lightly with turf and a layer of dust, and the bishop drove straight into it. He realised it was no accident, but persisted on foot. When he arrived, the reception was chilly, but he was offered a drink. He declined, and Froude helped himself to a large one. The bishop opened the conversation.

'I hear, Mr Froude, that you keep a pack of harriers.'

'Then you hear wrong, my lord. It is the pack that keeps me.'

'I do not understand.'

'They stock my larder with hares. You don't suppose I should have hares on my table unless they were caught for me? There's no butcher for miles and miles, and I can't get a joint but once in a fortnight. Forced to eat hares. And they must be caught to be eaten.'

The Bishop then said to Froude, 'I hear, sir, but I can hardly credit it, that you invite men to your house and keep them drinking and then fighting in your parlour.'

'My lord, you are misinformed. Don't believe a word of it. Directly they begins to fight and takes off their coats, I take 'em by the scruff of the neck and turns them out into the churchyard, and let 'em settle their differences among the tombs.'

Your lover or your pig?

Froude agreed to give his housekeeper a pig if she would give up her sweetheart, and continue to work for him. 'Which will you prefer now, Joe or the porker?' 'Lauk, sir, I'd rayther have the pig.'

But Froude suspected her of having her bacon and eating it, and one day he deliberately returned home unexpectedly when Joe was in the kitchen. Where to hide him? Where else, but in the great 'copper' used for laundry. Froude came into the room and looked about him. Something about the copper made him suspicious. On a pretext, he made his housekeeper fill the copper, pouring the water all over Joe, and then he made her light the fire, and stayed to watch. Joe bore it as manfully as a missionary in a cooking pot, but in the end there was no alternative but to leap out and make a dash for it.

With a wild hunting cry, Froude made after him with his horsewhip.

Mrs Russell's hounds

When Parson Jack Russell was over eighty he started keeping a pack of harriers. The Bishop of Exeter sent for him.

'Mr Russell, I hear you have got a pack of hounds. Is it so?'

'It is. I won't deny it , my lord.'

'Well, Mr Russell, it seems to me rather unsuitable for a clergyman to keep a pack. I do not ask you to give up hunting, for I know it would not be possible for you to exist without that. But will you, to oblige me, give up the pack?'

'Do y'ask it as a personal favour, my lord?'

'Yes, Mr Russell, as a personal favour.'

'Very well then, my lord, I will.'

'Thank you, thank you.' The Bishop, moved by his readiness,

held out his hand. 'Give me your hand, Mr Russell; you are – you really are – a good fellow.'

Jack Russell gave his great fist to the Bishop, who pressed it warmly. As they stood thus hand in hand, Jack said –

'I won't deceive you, not for the world, my lord. I'll give up the pack sure enough – but Mrs Russell will keep it instead of me.'

The Bishop dropped his hand.

Horse trading

Russell thought that in horse dealing, as in love and war, all things are lawful. It so happened that Parson Froude wanted a horse, and he asked his dear friend Russell if he knew where he could find one that was suitable. 'Would my brown horse do?' asked Russell. 'I want to sell him, because the hunting season is over and I have too many horses. Come into town on Saturday and dine with me in the middle of the day, and see the horse. If you like him, you can have him, and if you do not, there is no harm done.'

On Saturday, into South Molton came Froude. Russell lived there, as he was then curate of nearby Georgenympton. Froude stabled his horse at the lower end of the town. He was suspicious even of a friend, so, instead of going to Russell's lodging, he went to his stable and found the door locked. This circumstance made him more suspicious than ever, and, looking round, he saw a man on a ladder, from which he was thatching a cottage. He called to him for assistance, shifted the ladder to the stable, ascended and went by the 'tallet' door into the loft. He got down the steps inside, opened the window, and carefully inspected the horse, which he found to be suffering in both eyes from incipient cataract. He climbed back, got down the ladder, and shutting the window, went into a shop to have his coat brushed before he rang his friend's door-bell. The door was opened by Russell himself, who saluted him with: 'You are early Froude, come across to the bank with me for a moment, if you do not mind.'

In the street was standing a Combe Martin cart laden with early vegetables, and between the shafts was an old pony, stone blind, with glassy eyeballs. Froude paused, lifted the pony's head, turned its face to the light, looked at the white eyeballs and remarked, 'How blessed plenty blind horses there are in this town just now, Jack.'

Not another word was said. The dinner was eaten, the bottle of port wine was consumed, and Froude rode home without having been asked to see the brown horse. Russell knew the game was up, and that his little plan for making his friend view the horse after he had dined, and not before, had lamentably failed.

But that was the way with them. Froude would have dealt with his best friend in the same manner over horses.

Muscular Christianity

Froude's nephew Parson Radford of Lapford was a violent man. Indeed he was suspected of cutting the throat of a locum who was sent to replace him, when the bishop had suspended him from duty, and then terrorising the next locum into an early departure. At the boxing booths of South Molton Fair, Radford would give a prolonged exhibition of his powers, taking on one farm labourer after another. Once he invaded a camp of railway navvies, issued a challenge, and took on ten men in succession, each hoping that by now the cleric would be tiring. One Tolly, later a stationmaster, was the only man who ever stopped him.

When Radford was seen on the station platform on market day, local farmers bribed the guard to put him in a carriage by himself and lock the door, so fearful were they that he would challenge them to a fight.

The Hon. Newton Fellowes, later Lord Portsmouth, used to drive a four-in-hand and occasionally experienced trouble with carters who did not make room for him as fast as he thought proper, whom he would then punish with a slash of his whip. Radford had little hope of stopping this behaviour with sermonising, so one day he dressed up as a carter, and lying down in the cart pretended to be asleep. On came Newton Fellowes. Finding the carter apparently deaf to his commands, he flew into a perfect fury and began to flourish his whip. At the first touch, up jumped Radford, and administered to his lordship the worst drubbing he ever had in his life.

Tally-ho!

A parson was asked to officiate at a church east of South Molton, in the days when 'all kinds of music' made up a village choir. The psalm was announced, and the musicians began to tune their instruments. Unfortunately the fiddles and the bass viol would not be obliging, and some time elapsed before they were in accord. Impatient at the delay, the parson leant over the reading desk and, throwing his arms wildly above his head, shouted at the very top of his voice, 'Hark-away, Jack! hark-away, Jack! Tally-ho! Tally-ho!'

Time, gentlemen, please

The rector of Peter Tavy, the Rev. Mr McBean, would not start morning service until he was sure that none of the villagers were in the pub, which was right next to the churchyard. He used to send the churchwarden out to check on this. Now the churchwarden was a relative of the landlord, so his position was a delicate one. Being a man of peace, he hit upon a solution. As he walked across the churchyard, with his eyes fixed on the ground immediately in front of his toes, he repeated, getting louder as he approached, 'I'm coming, Cousin Tom, I'm coming, Cousin Tom.' At the door of the pub he would check that it was empty of customers – which it always was – and return to the church to report that the sermon could start. The vicar congratulated himself on his parishioners having such regard for the hours of worship.

Counting her chicks

Sir Lewis Pollard was a judge in Tudor times, and often obliged to be away from his home at King's Nympton. He left his wife in charge of preparing a stained glass window in the church, in which the couple were to appear accompanied by their children – of whom at the time there were no less than twenty-one. Lady Pollard, however, decided to have twenty-two children depicted, presuming that when her husband returned, there would be time for one more. Which, as Prince, the author of *Devon Worthies* says, 'inserted in expectation, came to pass in reality'.

Honi soit qui mal y pense

Prince Charles, later King Charles II, spent several weeks as a fugitive after the Royalist defeat at the Battle of Worcester. It was during this time that he escaped discovery by hiding in an oak tree. But he is said to have had an even narrower escape when, closely pursued, he sought refuge at Coaxdon House, near Axminster. Entering the parlour where the lady of the house, Mrs Cogan, was alone, he threw himself on her protection. It was then the fashion for ladies to wear large hoops, and as there was no time to be lost and the soldiers were even then entering the grounds, she instantly concealed him under her skirt.

Mrs Cogan was a royalist, but her husband was one of the opposite party, and was then out in his estate. When he saw the soldiers approaching the house, he joined them and they all walked into the room in which the lady was sitting, she affecting surprise at their intrusion. The men immediately announced their business, stating that as Prince Charles must be concealed upon the premises, they were authorised to make a strict search for him. Assenting with apparent readiness to their object, Mrs Cogan kept her seat while her husband accompanied them through every room in the house.

Being released from the immediate predicament, she was then able to provide for the security of the fugitive until it was prudent for him to depart, and furnished him with provisions and a change of clothes. He then left, and made his way to what was then the poor fishing village of Brightelmstone, now Brighton, and thence to France.

When in safety, Charles unsurprisingly remembered the incident, and sent her a handsome gold chain and locket. The order of the Garter would perhaps have been more appropriate.

There be a hand here as can strike

Another escape story of the Civil War concerns Henry Bidlake. Cromwell's troops surrounded Bidlake House, in order to capture him, but he was tipped off, and dressed himself in rags in order to pass them. Some of the soldiers met him, and asked whether he had seen Squire Bidlake. 'Aye, sure,' he replied, ''er was a-standin' on 's own doorstep a foo minutes agoo.' So they went on to search the house, while he escaped to the house of a tenant named Veale in Burleigh Wood. The troopers went there also, and Mrs Veale made him slide into the clock-case. They hunted high and low but could not find him. One of the soldiers, looking at the clock and seeing the hand at the hour, said 'What, doant he strike?' 'Aye, aye, mister,' replied Mrs Veale, 'there be a hand here as can strike, I tell 'ee.'

Mr Bidlake suffered from a chronic cough, and just at that moment he had the art to dip his head and let the weight down behind his back, so that the clock struck the hour and drowned the cough in the case.

Practical clockmanship

On an outlying farm the clock went wrong, and struck one at three, and two at four, and so on. This was a nuisance, as people were unable to remember which was wrong, the hands or the chimes. But the farmer settled it by keeping the clock an hour fast, and then, when it pointed to one and struck eleven, everyone knew it was twelve.

The stuff of which ghosts are made

A dining club used to meet at the 'Bunch of Grapes' in Kinterbury Street, Plymouth, and their president was one Humphrey

Tallent. One evening his chair was all too conspicuously empty, for he was lying at death's door. There was a general air of gloom in the normally convivial meeting, when suddenly the door flew open and a spectre, pale and ghastly, and dressed in dressing gown and nightcap, entered, and sat on a footstool. The company was speechless, until one, braver than the rest, ventured to say, 'I am glad to see you here again, sir. I hope you are better?'

The apparition only bowed, raised an empty glass and moved its lips in the toast of death, and withdrew, as silently as it had entered. When the general shock had passed, one of the members walked across to Mr Tallent's house, to enquire after his health and learned to his horror that he had just died. The faith of the members that they had seen his spirit at the point of his death was unshaken – until the nurse confessed that she fell asleep while attending the dying man, and found when she woke that he had left the room. In ten minutes he returned from the club, composed himself, and, exhausted by the effort, breathed his last.

An appetite for news

An old woman of seventy-five was to be photographed by an amateur. Nothing he said could persuade her to speak till the operation was completed. Then she put her finger into her mouth: 'You wouldn't ha' me took wi' my cheeks falled in? I just stuffed the *Western Marnin' News* in my mouth to fill'n out.'

Richard is himself again

The great actor Edmund Kean played in 'rep' at a theatre in Exeter before he became famous, and in his spare time taught fencing and elocution. The arty crowd of Exeter in his day congregated at the Turk's Head, in a room along a passage.

Kean is said to have left Exeter on foot, and returned in a coach and horses, but he had not forgotten his old friends. He ordered his coach to stop at the inn door, ran along the passage, burst into the room and, quoting his most famous part Richard III, leaped onto the table declaiming 'Richard's himself again!'

Wheel that boat!

When George Monk, later Duke of Albemarle and the key figure in the restoration of the Stuarts, first took employment under Oliver Cromwell, it was at sea against the Dutch. He had previously been a cavalry officer under Charles I. He performed good service, and was courageous enough, but he distinguished no better between the armed services than between rulers: instead of crying 'Tack about,' he would shout 'Wheel to the right!'

A snow white cloth

The village of Lydford was much neglected by its landlord and by its pluralist vicar. A poor curate officiated there, on a salary of £100 a year. One Christmas Day, the curate went to the church to celebrate Holy Communion and found the altar covered with snow that had blown in through the battered east window and under the cracked slates of the roof.

'I'll sweep it off,' said the clerk.

'On no account. God has spread his table,' said the curate; and he celebrated on the white sheet of snow.

The battle of the clerks

The clerk at Lydford was addicted to lifting his elbow too freely, and occasionally came to church in a hilarious condition. The climax was reached at a funeral, when he tumbled into the grave before the coffin, and addressed the dead man as he clambered out, 'Beg parding, Ted. I bain't minded to change places with you yet.'

The curate was obliged to dismiss him, and appoint another, Peter X.

The old clerk refused to accept his dismissal, and gathered his adherents. On the following Sunday he marched at their head to the house of God. Peter, forewarned of this and having the keys, seated himself early in the clerk's pew, surrounded by his own supporters. The rival party entered and a battle ensued . The curate absolutely refused to perform the service to the clerking of the dismissed official and finally the latter and his gang were ejected from the church, loudly professing that they would turn dissenters.

Moor dalliance

A married couple, holidaying in Chagford with a young lady who was their guest, had gone for a drive on the moor in their gig. The young lady expressed a wish to climb to the top of a tor. The wife said she would look after the horse, so up went the husband and the girl, while the wife walked the horse along the road to where they would descend, a little further along the road. They reached the top of the tor, waved vigorously and started the descent. But the path suddenly entered a morass. Searching for a way out, they walked backward and forward, and every now and then he extended his hand to help her from one tuft to another. They came down, went up, turned and got more involved in the bog, came down again, and they were fully half an hour in that morass.

Meanwhile, the wife paced up and down the road, glaring at her husband and the girl, dallying on the moor as she took it. Her pace quickened, her about-turns became sharper, her glances grew more indignant minute by minute. She saw them approach, then retrace their steps, gyrate, nearly fall into each other's arms, hold hands, and then walk straight down the slope towards a point well away from her.

Along the road paced the lady, flourishing her parasol at them. She called but they paid her no attention; they had their heads down and were clearly deep in conversation. Finally they were out of the swamp, and came confidently down towards her, laughing cheerfully at their shared adventure. The lady was speechless with wrath.

The observer of all this was Sabine Baring-Gould, who covertly followed the party to the inn where they subsequently took tea. There was a good spread but the husband had no appetite, and even the young lady was subdued. Presently they drove away, the lady brandishing the whip, the girl beside her, and the husband huddled in the back, disconsolate and suffering.

After the PM's neck

Lord North, then a far from popular Prime Minister, was staying at Ashe at harvest time in 1765. He heard from a neighbouring field the reapers 'crying the neck', and saw them waving their sickles in the air. Not knowing of this ancient custom, when the reapers dedicated the last sheaf to the spirit of the harvest, he was convinced that they were after his own neck. His fears were communicated to his friend Sir Robert Hamilton, who drew his sword and rushed into the midst of the astonished labourers. The misunderstanding was soon sorted out and the sword returned bloodless to its scabbard.

Ironically, Lord North's instinct may have been correct, for it is conjectured that the ancient custom may be the relic of a human sacrifice, where the first passing stranger was seized and killed to propitiate the gods.

Snails house

Below Lough Tor (Laughter Tor on Ordnance Survey maps) is a cottage once known as White Slade, but nicknamed Snails House in Victorian times. Here there lived two spinsters, plump and healthy, but with no visible means of subsistence. No food was ever seen to enter their door, and they kept no poultry or livestock. Dark suspicions arose. How did these ladies live? Was it on Dartmoor mutton, stolen and brought to the house at dead of night? So a posse of moor-folk visited the house, and strangely they were admitted willingly to make a search. For a time nothing edible could be found – then, triumph! – certain pans were discovered and dragged forth excitedly. Disappointment! Salted slugs!

But curiously, after this the two ladies gradually pined away, till there were no more miserable-looking creatures upon the moor.

Put not your trust in parsons

In 1628 a labourer named Humphrie Hutchins was working in the fields high above Farway church when he found a cache of gold coins, together with an aged parchment. Being unable to read, Humphrie took it to the parson, Thomas Foster, who informed him that it stated that the finder must spend as much money as was necessary to repair the church before keeping the balance for himself. Humphrie did as the parson said; the place where he found the hoard is called Money Acre Corner and Humphrie's bust sits in a niche in the north aisle of the church.

Put not your trust in estate agents

A vicar of Talaton hated dissenters. He heard that a plot of land in the village was for sale, and that the dissenters were after it to build a chapel, so he bought it himself at a high price. News of this got around, and whenever any piece of land came on the market it was rumoured that the dissenters were after it. The rector and his purse rose to every occasion!

A unique event

The parson of Blackborough announced to his sparse congregation that if they would come to church next Sunday, they would see something they had never seen before in their lives. They came, and the rest of the parish came, and he remarked that neither he nor they had ever seen their church so full. One may doubt whether it was ever full again afterwards.

Worm turns

Sir Marc Brunel (father of the more famous Isambard Kingdom Brunel, but a fine engineer in his own right) was contemplating the problem of putting a the tunnel under the Thames at Wapping, when he happened to visit a Devon dockyard and there observed a creature with a peculiar head, boring steadily into a large timber. 'Eureka,' said Brunel, 'you are the fellow for me.' It was the teredo worm, and Brunel constructed something very like it – a tunnelling shield, patented in 1818 – with which he was able to construct his tunnel.

The bride's gloves

A stout buxom girl was getting married, around 1850 it must have been. When the ring was called for, she could not get her glove off, for the weather was warm and the party had walked to church. The bride tugged, the bridegroom tugged, her father tugged, but the thing would not come off.

'Why do you wear 'em, my dear?' said the officiating clergy-man. 'Are you afraid your hands will wear out? I am more than seventy years of age, and I have never worn such things, and look! my hands are not worn out yet!'

Another dish of tay?

Dr Johnson visited Plymouth, and was much impressed, both by the naval dockyard and the local produce. One day he indulged so heavily at dinner in honey, clotted cream and new cider that his friends feared for his life. But the man who could drink nineteen cups of tea (at a time when it cost two guineas a pound) was hardly likely to restrain himself over such homely luxuries as honey, cream and cider. It is said that his hostess ironically asked him whether he would care for the twentieth cup. As the Doctor gruffly responded in the affirmative, she rang the bell and told the servant to bring a bucket from the stable.

Such was his renown that a local alderman came to consult him on an important question. The 'Dockers', or inhabitants of the town which was then called Dock and is now Devonport, were suffering from a drought, and were pleading to be allowed some of Plymouth's excess water. The alderman showed by the way he put the question that he opposed allowing this, and Dr Johnson, with heavy irony, replied, 'I'd let the rogues die of thirst, for I hate a Docker from my heart.' The alderman joyful-ly reported back to the his Council colleagues that the great Dr Johnson shared his opinion entirely.

Winstanley's wish come true

When Henry Winstanley, 'the Merlin of his age', was building his fanciful and audacious lighthouse on the Eddystone rock, England was at war with France. A French privateer surprised the working party, while the ship which should have protected them (the aptly named HMS *Terrible*) was neglecting its duties. The French took a few pot-shots for amusement, then landed and took Winstanley captive, although they left the workmen.

When King Louis found out, he was horrified and ordered Winstanley released immediately. He said he was 'at war with England and not with humanity,' and apologised in person to the inventor.

Winstanley was a genius at self-publicising, and this incident was a gift. Before long everyone in England had heard of the obscure but lethal reef.

The light was lit on 14 November 1698. The outside of the lighthouse was already festooned with cranes and ornamental candelabra, but Winstanley had added 'a moving engine trough to cast down stones to defend the landing stage in case of need'. However, he had reckoned without HMS *Terrible*, which press-ganged the only boatman in Plymouth able and willing to land supplies on the rock, so the keepers nearly starved before he could effect the man's release.

Winstanley had total confidence in his pioneering structure, and expressed the wish to be in it 'during the greatest storm that ever was'. By chance, he was. The storm of 26 November 1703 was a misplaced hurricane which did incredible damage across the whole of England. On land, it totally destroyed a thousand or more houses and four hundred windmills. At sea, the Royal Navy alone lost thirteen ships, many smaller craft, and some two thousand men drowned. Winstanley and his keepers were swept away, and there was scarcely any trace of the building by the time the storm blew itself out .

Taking the lead

The second Eddystone lighthouse lasted rather longer than Winstanley's, and was destroyed by fire rather than by storm, in 1755. One of the surviving keepers was aged 94. After being burned in the fire, then awaiting rescue on the wave-swept rock for several hours and finally – because it was too rough to land a boat – being dragged off through the waves on a rope's end, he was thought to have lost his wits when he claimed to have accidentally swallowed some of the molten lead from the roof. He appeared to be recovering, then suddenly relapsed after twelve days, and died. Had he really swallowed lead after all? The doctor knew only one way to find out. An autopsy revealed in his stomach a flat piece of lead weighing 200 grams, and over ten centimetres across.

A living proportionable to his mind

The Earl of Devon gave the substantial rectory of Tiverton to his chaplain, who lived for some time there on its income, but well beyond his means. He would complain to his lord's officers about his general lack of money, and sometimes more specifically, that the living did not produce the income needed to entertain in a style appropriate to someone of his standing.

As he spoke often in this way, it came to the attention of the Earl, who invited his former chaplain to come and discuss his complaint. He told the parson that he had considered the matter and that he intended 'to procure him a living more proportionable to his mind and convenience', if at some stage he would first care to resign his present living.

The incumbent, encouraged by these words and in the hope of higher promotion, handed in his immediate resignation. Whereupon the Earl explained that he intended to divide the living of Tiverton into four parts, Prior, Tidcombe, Clare and Pitt, and to bestow these smaller livings on four separate men. But out of respect to his former chaplain, and former incumbent, he would offer him the first choice.

Seeing his lordship's intent, and being without any other great connection from which might hope for preferment, he accepted gratefully, 'and thereby was fairly taught to live by a crown who could not live by a pound.'

No modern personnel director could have managed it better.

Devon's old roads

When the first Turnpike Act in Devon was applied for, its proposer in the Commons said it would in fact be no more expensive to make the roads navigable under a Navigation Act than to make them fit for carriages under a Turnpike Act, so much water already lay in them.

Admiral Duckworth seized by the Devil

The Royal Navy was renowned for its harsh discipline, but Admiral Duckworth had a reputation for being harsher than most. A few nights after he died, in 1817, a sentry created an alarm by firing his gun in the air. The guard turned out, and the sentry was placed under arrest. He explained that he had shot at the ghost of the Admiral as it was hurried away by a dark figure.

Fortunately for him there was proof that this was so, since a mess steward had heard the clock strike thirteen just as the shot was fired.

Espionage

In the 1740s, Tiverton, formerly a major cloth manufacturing town, began to lose its main Dutch market. This was not because of the industrial revolution, which had not then got fully under way, but because the type of coarse cloth produced in Tiverton was held in lower esteem than new types of cloth produced in Norwich – 'camblets, tarborates, damasks, barragons, lutestrings, calamancoes, tarbines' and other exotic stuffs. Men were laid off and factories closed in Tiverton, and it led to riots and tumults in the town, especially when Irish wool was imported and the wool-combers lost their livelihood.

One of the leading firms was that of Mrs Enchmarch & Sons (for there were many successful businesswomen in the eighteenth century) and Mrs Enchmarch sent one of her sons to Norwich, with a weaver named William Perkins. They remained there some time to make themselves fully acquainted with the plans of the woollen manufacturers there. They had almost completed their industrial espionage, when their purpose was suspected, and it was with great difficulty and hazard that they escaped from the city. Had they fallen into the hands of their pursuers, it would probably have cost them their lives.

The jester's view of hell

John Arscott of Tetcott (1718-1783) was a country squire of the kind described by Fielding in *Tom Jones*. He kept possibly the last dwarf jester in England, Black John. One evening Black John fell asleep by the hearth in the hall at Tetcott. Suddenly he started up with a cry, 'Oh, master, I was in a sog [sleep] and I thought I was dead and in hell.'

'Well, John,' said the squire, 'and what did you see there?'

'Sir, everything very much like what it is here in Tetcott Hall, the gentlefolks nearest the fire.'

The diving belle

Sir Alexander Harty descended in his own experimental diving bell, but had such discomfort in his ears that he could not remain below. His daughter then took his place, and accomplished the work they had undertaken. She sent up a note in verse:

> From a belle, my dear, you've oft had a line,
> But not from a bell under water.
> Just now I can only assure you I'm thine,
> Your diving, affectionate daughter.

The printing parson

William Davy (1743-1826), curate of Moreton, Lustleigh and Drewsteignton, was a prolific sermon-writer. He could not find a publisher for them, so bought a printing press and printed 26 large volumes by hand, 500 sermons in all. His 'print-run' was just 14 copies! The writing and printing perhaps became obsessive: when his son displeased him, he printed a pamphlet condemning his behaviour. His son had the last laugh, being invited to write a memoir of his father after his death, in which he repaid the unkindness with interest.

Coming up trumps

A vicar of Moreton was playing whist one evening in a country house when he had a heart attack while dealing. The standard Edwardian remedies were applied, hartshorn, burnt feathers, and so on, and he recovered. Everybody looked at him, as people do in such circumstances, perhaps waiting for some word of the great beyond. 'What's trumps,' he asked quietly.

Daughter Olive

When Cecil Torr (who wrote the wonderfully entertaining *Small Talk at Wreyland*) found that some of his neighbours had never seen olives, he gave them some from the tree in his garden. One commented, 'Well, Mrs —'d never have christened her daughter Olive, if her'd a-tasted one of they.'

The humbling church

Richard Polwhele comments in his *History of Devonshire* that the inhabitants of Brent Tor, where the church is on top of a steep 300 metre hill, make weekly atonement for their sins: for they can never go to church without the previous penance of climbing up this steep hill, which they are often obliged to attempt, in the lowliest attitude. In windy or rainy weather, the worthy pastor himself is frequently obliged to humble himself on all fours, preparatory to his being exalted in the pulpit.

Lustleigh Flower Show, 1900, by an eye-witness

We went in about two, when it opened, and found some disorder in the main tent, as it had partially blown down earlier. Then there was a horrible noise, and the wind ripped the poultry tent almost in half. The whole thing began to collapse, men were rushing in and being pulled out by screaming females, some were tightening ropes, which others immediately loosened, and presently a great flap of canvas overturned the whole stand of cages – a horrid mass of ducks and fowls screaming and quacking and flapping all over the crowd, pursued by their owners and upsetting everything. And just at this moment the big flower marquee – which was of course deserted – was caught by a tremendous puff of wind and torn right up and dropped on the tables inside. It wasn't heavy enough to be dangerous, but I wish I could give you an idea of how funny it was to see ——, who was rather bossing the show, creep from under the canvas with an old lady, an infuriated fowl pecking at his knickerbocker calves. One of the nicest incidents was a little old lady in a velvet mantle and black curls, careering backward over the ground, knocking people over as she clutched at the tail of a huge escaping and crowing cock with one hand, and with the other arm embraced a captured but still struggling and squawking goose. In about an hour after it opened everything on the ground was swept quite flat. But excursion trains kept arriving, whose innocent passengers paid their sixpences – you couldn't see the ruin from outside – and wondered why the crowd assembled at the gate laughed at them.

Rural devil

There is a famous story that the devil destroyed Widecombe church when he caught a sinner napping (the church was dramatically struck by lightning in 1638 during a service) and that the devil had stopped on his way across the moor to Widecombe and asked for water at a remote cottage. A woman living in that same cottage two hundred years later saw a tall man dressed in black, on a great black stallion, loom out of the fog, and ask for water. It was in fact the rural dean, but she fled before discovering this. She said it was his horns which had convinced her.

Church losses

For centuries people have been gradually deserting the church of England, often for doctrinal reasons, but not always. One elderly lady did so because her grandchild had caught its death of cold through the parson 'a-baptizin' it without a-puttin' a kettleful o' bilin' water into that stoney font.'

'Why tarry the wheels of his charabanc?' (Judges, 5,28)

Charabancs are known in Devon as 'cherubim'. On venturing to hint that this was a mistake, I got a crushing reply: "Why, us read of the Lord a-ridin' on the wings of the Cherubim, and they folk be a-ridin' on their seats.' [Cecil Torr]

The nutty ghost

Old Mother Elston used to go from place to place selling nuts, and before she died she begged that a bag of them should be put in her coffin. Her wishes were fulfilled when she was buried. Then it began to be said that her ghost used to sit on her grave and crack nuts. Many people had heard it, and the clergyman of the parish was told. He said that if at any time its presence was made known to him, he would come at once and lay it.

One fine night, after a neighbouring 'revel' [parish feast day], three men rather the worse for drink came by, and saw some sheep in a field close to the churchyard. The thought struck them that this was a good opportunity for helping themselves. While one man went to the porch to keep watch, the others went off to steal the sheep. Now the man in the porch had brought a lot of nuts from the revel, and while waiting he began to eat them. Just then, the sexton came by, heard the nuts being cracked and immediately ran to the vicarage to fetch the parson, who agreed to come at once.

Unfortunately he was afflicted with St Vitus' Dance and could not walk, being dependent on a wheelchair. But the wheelchair could not immediately be found.

'Never mind, for this little distance you can carry me on your back,' said the parson. So off they went and just inside the churchyard they heard the nuts still being cracked. The sexton stopped. 'Go a little nearer,' said the parson. The sexton went a little nearer. 'A little nearer still,' he urged and the sexton edged closer. Then the parson began to speak some words to lay the ghost.

But the man in the porch, seeing the silhouette of the vicar on the sexton's shoulders, thought it was one of his mates returning with a sheep. 'Is he fat?' he called. The sexton was so frightened that he dropped the parson and ran away as fast as he could. But just as fright brings on St Vitus' Dance, so it can cure it, and from that time the vicar could walk as well as ever he could.

> 'Whoever reads these stories, and then
> lives an hundred years,
> shall not die young.'

THE END